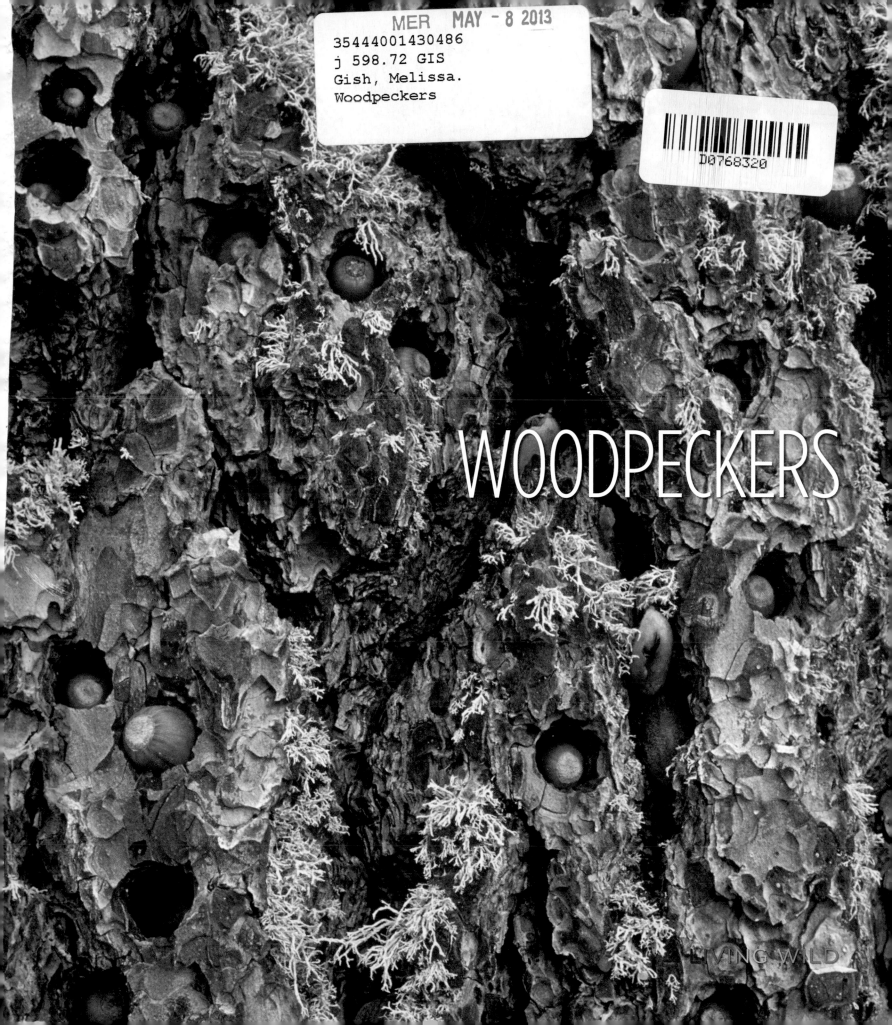

WOODPECKERS

LIVING WILD

LIVING WILD

Published by Creative Paperbacks
P.O. Box 227, Mankato, Minnesota 56002
Creative Paperbacks is an imprint of The Creative Company
www.thecreativecompany.us

Design and production by Mary Herrmann
Art direction by Rita Marshall
Printed in the United States of America

Photographs by Alamy (Stuart Clarke, William Leaman, Rolf Nussbaumer Photography, jack thomas), Corbis (Araldo de Luca, Heritage Images), Dreamstime (Rinus Baak, Cammeraydave, Epstefanov, David Maixner, Mirceax, Ron Chapple Studios, Simplyzel, Trishz, Victortyakht), Flickr (Somchai Kanchanasut), Getty Images (After John James Audubon, Gary Meszaros, NASA/Hulton Archive, Pete Oxford, Frank Schneidermeyer), iStockphoto (Robin Arnold, Robert Blanchard, Steve Byland, Bryan Eastham, eROMAZe, Ronald Glovan, Georgios Kollidas, kumakuma1216, Frank Leung, Liz Leyden, Richard Lindie, Daniel Parent, Dieter Spears, Michael Thompson, Vassiliy Vishnevskiy, Wildpix 645), CK Leong, National Aviary; National Museum of the American Indian, Smithsonian Institution [20/9651]; Shutterstock (FotoVeto, Brendan Howard, Martha Marks, Ron Rowan Photography, Vishnevskiy Vasily), Superstock (Belinda Images)

Library of Congress Cataloging-in-Publication Data
Gish, Melissa.
Woodpeckers / by Melissa Gish.
p. cm. — (Living wild)
Includes bibliographical references and index.
Summary: A look at woodpeckers, including their habitats, physical characteristics such as their hammering beaks, behaviors, relationships with humans, and protected status in the world today.
ISBN 978-1-60818-172-8 (hardcover)
ISBN 978-0-89812-779-9 (pbk)
1. Woodpeckers—Juvenile literature. I. Title.

QL696.P56G57 2012
598.7'2—dc23   2011035796

First Edition
9 8 7 6 5 4 3 2 1

WOODPECKERS

Melissa Gish

On a cool October morning, in southwestern
Colorado's San Juan National Forest, a group of

birds with black backs, white bellies, and brilliant
red caps flits among a stand of ponderosa pines.

On a cool October morning, on a mountainside in southwestern Colorado's San Juan National Forest, a group of birds with black backs, white bellies, and brilliant red caps flits among a stand of ponderosa pines. The birds are acorn woodpeckers. They are busily preparing for winter, gathering acorns from white oaks farther up the mountain and carrying them in their beaks to the pines below. Clinging to the side of a tree 40 feet (12 m) above the ground, a

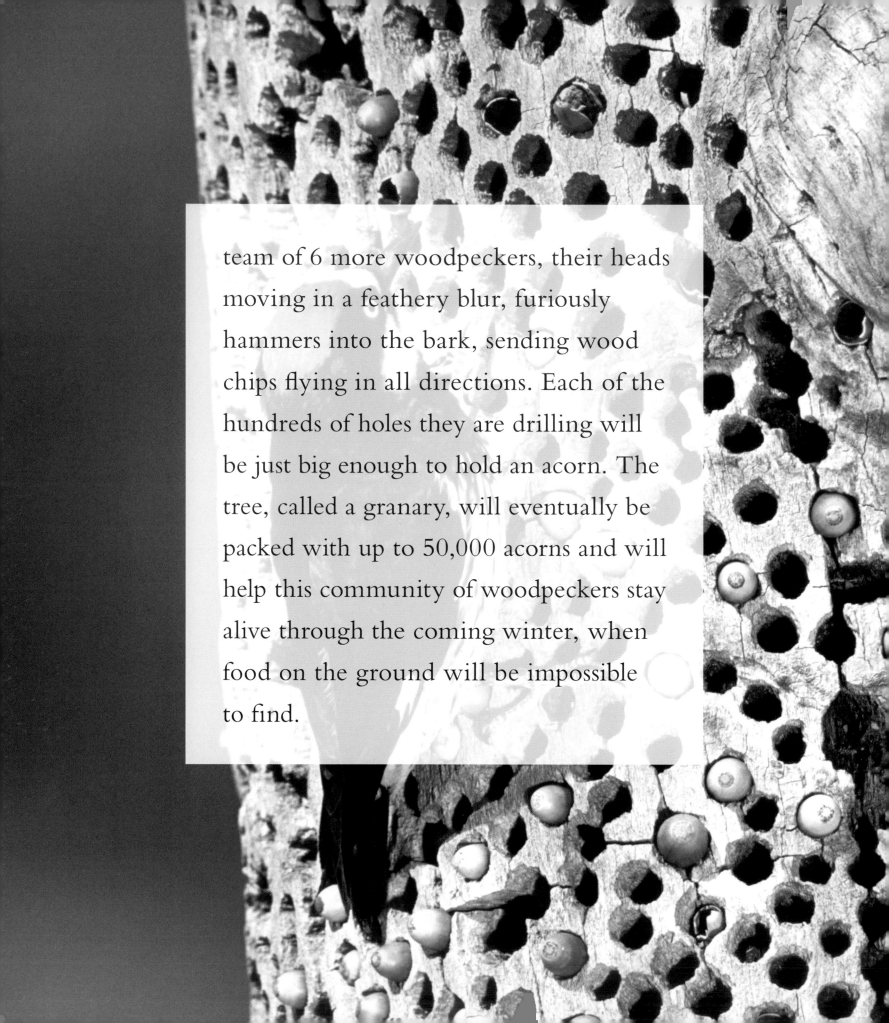

team of 6 more woodpeckers, their heads moving in a feathery blur, furiously hammers into the bark, sending wood chips flying in all directions. Each of the hundreds of holes they are drilling will be just big enough to hold an acorn. The tree, called a granary, will eventually be packed with up to 50,000 acorns and will help this community of woodpeckers stay alive through the coming winter, when food on the ground will be impossible to find.

WHERE IN THE WORLD THEY LIVE

■ **Northern Flicker (Red-shafted)** western North America

■ **Rufous-headed Woodpecker** western Amazon basin

■ **Pileated Woodpecker** Canada, eastern United States, Pacific Coast

Gila Woodpecker southwestern United States

Nubian Woodpecker central and eastern Africa

Black-headed Woodpecker Southeast Asia

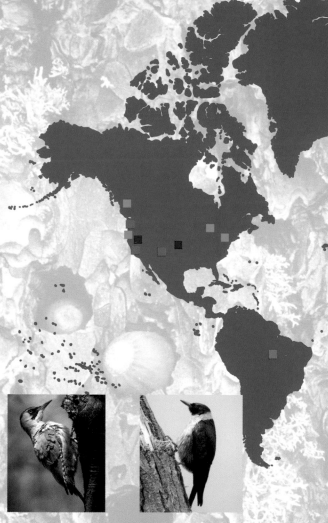

■ **Green Woodpecker** Europe

■ **Lewis's Woodpecker** western to central United States

There are approximately 180 species of woodpecker, flicker, and sapsucker living in the world today. Primarily forest-dwelling birds (though some inhabit deserts and rocky hillsides), they are found in the Americas, Europe, Asia, and Africa, with some migrating to warmer climes during the winter months. The eight species shown here represent the diversity of the birds' range.

BUG-BUSTING BIRDS

The Asian pygmy woodpecker, an active bird usually found on higher branches, is smaller than a sparrow.

Woodpeckers are some of the most distinctive birds on the planet. Powerful necks and strong beaks allow these energetic birds to bore through tree trunks, utility poles, and even the sides of houses like mini power drills. Of the 225 species in the family Picidae, 183 belong to the subfamily Picinae—the true woodpeckers—and consist of the woodpeckers, flickers, and sapsuckers. The other members of Picidae are wrynecks and piculets, birds that are typically smaller than true woodpeckers but also peck wood.

Woodpeckers are mainly woodland birds and are found everywhere on Earth except in Arctic and Antarctic regions, Madagascar, and Australia and its neighboring islands. They range in size from Asia's 5-inch (12.7 cm) pygmy woodpecker to North America's 23-inch (58.4 cm) imperial woodpecker. The imperial woodpecker is currently categorized by the International Union for Conservation of Nature (IUCN) as critically endangered. Researchers believe this bird may be **extinct** because the last official sighting was in 1956. Despite an unconfirmed sighting in Arkansas in 2005 of the

A group of woodpeckers is called a drumming or a gatling, the latter of which refers to the sound made by a rapid-fire Gatling gun.

Due to habitat loss, the great slaty woodpecker is listed as vulnerable on the IUCN Red List of Threatened Species.

Scientists believe Lewis's woodpecker populations may have declined by as much as 50 percent since the mid-1960s.

second-largest woodpecker, the 20-inch (50.8 cm) ivory-billed woodpecker, that species is also believed to be extinct. This leaves the great slaty woodpecker of Southeast Asia, nearly the size of the ivory-billed woodpecker, as the largest *confirmed* species of woodpecker in the world.

Most woodpeckers have black, white, gray, or brown feathers, with rows of spots or hash marks on their backs, tails, or undersides. This pattern, called a "ladder," distinguishes virtually all woodpeckers from other birds. Many woodpeckers have red, orange, or yellow markings on their bodies or heads. With its greenish-black **plumage** and pink breast, the Lewis's woodpecker, named for explorer Meriwether Lewis, is one of the most colorful woodpeckers in North America. In several species, males have markings that females lack. The males of some species are larger than females and have longer tails and beaks as well. Such differences in body size and coloration between males and females indicate what is known as sexual dimorphism.

Woodpeckers have short legs, and each foot has two toes that point forward and two that point backward. These strong toes, which have sharp claws, allow

Unlike most other woodpeckers that search beneath bark, Lewis's woodpeckers eat insects on the surface of trees.

The red-headed woodpecker is the only woodpecker that stores food by hiding it with bark or wood.

woodpeckers to cling to trees vertically. Their tail feathers, the stiffest of any bird's, provide balance and leverage when woodpeckers do what they do best—peck wood. Woodpeckers use their powerful neck muscles to rap against surfaces up to 28 times per second. A woodpecker's beak is made of keratin—the same material found in human fingernails—but it also contains a strong bone that moves slightly to absorb the shock of each hard peck. Woodpeckers have especially thick spinal bones that act as shock absorbers, protecting the back and neck, and a thick skull that cushions the brain, shielding it from damage as the bird drums.

Woodpeckers, like all birds, are warm-blooded. This means they are able to keep their body temperature at a constant level, no matter what the temperature is outside. Birds may adjust their body temperatures by panting to cool down or shivering to warm up. They also fluff up their feathers to create air pockets that help **insulate** them against cold weather. When they fly, woodpeckers flap their wings a few times for lift and then fold in their wings to drift. A woodpecker's undulating, up-and-down flight is easy to recognize.

The black woodpecker flies in a straight line instead of following the dipping pattern of other woodpeckers.

A woodpecker's toe arrangement, with two pointing forward and two pointing backward, is described as zygodactyl.

Woodpeckers eat a variety of foods. Most species hunt insects that live on or inside trees. Their favorite insects are ants; in fact, in North America, woodpeckers eat more ants than any other bird because their stomachs contain acids that **neutralize** the chemical irritants that ants carry in their bodies. A few species of woodpecker, such as the northern flicker and Lewis's woodpecker, snatch flying insects from the air, and the acorn woodpecker feeds on acorns, collecting them all summer and storing them for the winter in holes drilled in trees. Sapsuckers are named for their practice of eating sap that drips from the holes they drill in trees, and the desert-dwelling Gila woodpecker eats cactus fruits. Many woodpeckers supplement their diets with nuts, seeds, and berries. Some species, such as the red-headed woodpecker, even eat bird eggs and mice.

Like most birds, woodpeckers have a poor sense of smell, so they hunt for insects using their keen hearing. Drumming on tree bark causes insects and their immature offspring, called larvae, to move beneath the surface. A woodpecker will drum, pause to listen for the location of its prey, and then drum again, if necessary, to create an opening through which it can probe for prey.

Woodpeckers such as the great spotted (pictured) use their stiff tails as support while drilling for insects.

While searching for carpenter ants in young trees, pileated woodpeckers may drill holes so large that the trees break apart.

Woodpeckers have the longest tongues of any bird—up to four inches (10 cm). All birds have a series of slender bones, called hyoid horns, that extends from strong muscles on either side of the lower jaw. The tongue is anchored at a point called the hyoid apparatus. However, in woodpeckers, the entire tongue consists of the hyoid apparatus—a long string of tiny bones covered in muscle and soft tissue. This makes the woodpecker's tongue stiff. Also, the tongue grows longer as the woodpecker ages, eventually curling around the back of the skull and into the right nostril. Flexing the jaw muscles causes the tongue to snap tight and extend from the woodpecker's beak.

After a woodpecker has chiseled off a layer of tree bark or made a hole, it will stick its beak into the crevice and use its sensitive tongue to search for and then spear food. The tongue is equipped with a sticky covering that works like glue and backward-pointing barbs, resembling tiny fishhooks, which allow the woodpecker to pull the creature out of its hiding place. The tongue is retracted while the woodpecker drills holes, and the nostrils, which are narrow slits set on the sides of the beak, are protected from flying sawdust and debris by bristly feathers.

Woodpeckers make their homes in live trees, dead trees (called snags), or structures such as chimneys, buildings, or man-made nest boxes. As natural excavators, woodpeckers provide a valuable service to their **ecosystems**. No other bird can bore into trees and other surfaces the way a woodpecker can. Woodpecker holes provide homes for many creatures, including owls and other birds, mice, squirrels, and even bees.

The lesser golden-backed woodpecker of Asia uses its long tongue to reach insects and feed its young.

Gila woodpeckers, distinct for their zebra-like coloration, are also known for their long and steady drumming patterns.

NATURE'S PERCUSSIONISTS

Depending on the species, woodpeckers typically live from 4 to 11 years. However, some exceptions have been recorded. The Patuxent Wildlife Research Center in Laurel, Maryland, studies bird longevity by monitoring birds that have been banded. The center banded an acorn woodpecker in 1992 and then recorded it 17 years later—discovering that this was the longest-lived woodpecker on record.

Woodpeckers reach maturity and are ready to mate at one year old. Most woodpecker species are monogamous, meaning they remain with the same mate throughout the mating season, which typically begins in February or March. Sometimes partners return to each other the following year. To attract a mate, woodpeckers announce their presence in a territory by drumming loudly and continuously on surfaces such as dead trees or utility poles. These surfaces create an echo that can be heard over long distances. While woodpeckers typically drum a few dozen times a day most of the year, they may drum 8,000 to 12,000 times a day during mating season. Both males and females call to each other by drumming.

In the southwestern U.S. and Mexico, Gila woodpeckers nest inside giant saguaro cacti, where they can escape the desert heat.

Woodpeckers native to warmer places may lay up to three clutches of eggs per breeding season.

Most woodpeckers follow a distinctive flying pattern that consists of flapping three times, then gliding, then repeating.

As part of their courtship, woodpeckers fly past each other to show off their feathers. Healthy feathers show that a potential mate has a good chance of producing healthy offspring. When two woodpeckers form a pair bond, they will typically use the male's current roost for the nest site. They indicate agreement on the nest site by lightly drumming on its surface together. This is called mutual tapping. Woodpeckers never use the same nest site twice.

Both mates share in the work of enlarging the roost to make room for the nest, drilling the hole deeper and carrying debris away. Unlike other birds, woodpeckers do not use twigs, mud, or feathers to make a nest. Rather, they simply leave some wood chips in the bottom of the hole as soft padding. It often takes up to three weeks to prepare the nest. During this time, the pair also protects their territory from competing woodpeckers and intruders, such as owls, that may try to invade their nest cavity.

Female woodpeckers that live in warm climates, such as the laced woodpecker of Southeast Asia, lay one to three eggs at a rate of one egg per day. Species that live in cooler climates, such as the northern flicker, lay four to nine eggs at a time. A group of eggs is called a clutch.

The white eggs are 0.6 to 1.3 inches (1.5–3.3 cm) long, depending on the species.

Like all birds' eggs, woodpecker eggs must be incubated, or kept warm, while the baby birds are developing inside. Both parents participate in the task of incubation. During the day, the female gently sits in the nest with the eggs situated under her breast and wings. At night, the male takes over, and the female returns to her own roost. Small

The great spotted woodpecker lays a clutch of five to seven eggs and eats acorns when other food is scarce.

Young woodpeckers may out-grow their nest cavity and have to move out even before they are fully fledged.

The rufous hummingbird commonly follows the red-breasted sapsucker, feeding at the sap wells drilled by the sapsucker.

woodpeckers incubate their eggs for 11 to 14 days, but larger species, such as pileated woodpeckers and gilded flickers, must incubate their eggs for 16 to 18 days, after which time the baby woodpeckers hatch.

A baby woodpecker begins to chirp inside its egg two hours before hatching. Using its **egg tooth**, the hatchling chips through the hard shell of its egg. Some species, including the red-bellied woodpecker, have two egg teeth, one on the upper beak and one on the lower beak. The tiny bird is helpless once hatched; its eyes are closed, and its body is featherless. Within hours, some species begin to gobble up bits of berries and insect larvae carried to them by their parents. Other species swallow liquefied food that their parents bring back up directly into the nestlings' mouths. Stronger offspring often get the most food, pushing their siblings aside.

Although woodpecker parents are naturally vigilant, predators often raid nests. Squirrels, snakes, and other birds may steal eggs or hatchlings. If this occurs in the spring, a woodpecker pair may mate again and lay a second clutch; however, if they lose their babies during the summer, the woodpeckers will give up until the following year.

Woodpecker hatchlings grow quickly. Within 8 to 10 days, their eyes open, and their first feathers emerge. Young woodpeckers are strong enough to **fledge** when they are 20 to 35 days old. Tropical woodpeckers, which form family groups of 20 or more individuals, may remain in the nest for an additional 3 months to bond with their parents and siblings. While young woodpeckers instinctively poke their beaks under bark to hunt for food, most do not begin hammering holes into wood until they are three to four months old. Until they drill a roost inside a tree or other structure, young woodpeckers are vulnerable and suffer from a high **mortality rate**. Harsh weather, lack of food, and predators such as hawks and owls all threaten woodpeckers in the first few months of life on their own.

In cold climates, where winters can be harsh and food scarce, many woodpeckers **migrate** to warmer locations. If food is available, however, woodpeckers will stay in the same place year round. More than half of young northern woodpeckers that struggle through their first winter perish. In warmer climates, the birds have a much better chance of finding enough food to survive.

Like many birds, woodpecker parents partially digest food and then regurgitate it directly into their offspring's mouths.

Woodpeckers dependent on restricted food sources—such as certain seeds or sap—are most affected by logging.

Golden-fronted woodpeckers of Oklahoma and Texas are beneficial to farmers there because they eat pesky grasshoppers.

Even as adults, woodpeckers may fall victim to predators and competitors. While woodpeckers' speckled markings provide **camouflage**, sharp-eyed raptors such as red-tailed hawks and American kestrels regularly prey on woodpeckers. Additionally, aggressive birds such as starlings and owls may force woodpeckers out of their roosts. Even larger woodpeckers may take over the territory of smaller woodpeckers sometimes.

By far, the greatest threat to woodpeckers is human interference. Woodpeckers thrive where trees are dead, hammering into the soft flesh of decaying wood to retrieve insects and larvae. When people cut down or burn out dead trees during lumber operations or to make room for urban development, valuable woodpecker habitats are destroyed. Forced into areas where trees are too hard to hammer or too short to provide proper nest sites, woodpeckers cannot survive.

Such destruction and displacement has greatly reduced the numbers of many woodpecker species and even driven the two largest woodpeckers—the imperial and ivory-billed species—to probable extinction.

When John James Audubon painted these ivory-billed woodpeckers in 1829, the species was abundant in the U.S.

THE WOODPECKER

His bill an auger is,

His head, a cap and frill.

He laboreth at every tree,—

A worm his utmost goal.

by Emily Dickinson (1830–86)

KNOCK ON WOOD

S ince ancient times, the woodpecker has been included in stories and legends. In Greek **mythology**, Celeus was a man who, along with three companions, tried to steal honey from a sacred cave on Mount Ida, where Zeus, the king of all gods, was born. Zeus punished Celcus and his cohorts by turning them all into birds. Celeus was turned into a green woodpecker. This myth led to the naming of the genus Celeus, which contains 11 tropical woodpeckers such as the brilliantly colored rufous-headed and Kaempfer's woodpeckers.

In Roman mythology, Saturn was the god of agriculture, and his son, Picus, was the god of the forests. Circe, a goddess well known for her use of potions and herbs, fell in love with Picus and tried to steal him from his wife. But Picus could not be lured away. Circe, angered by Picus's rejection of her, created a potion that transformed Picus into a woodpecker. He was cursed to peck at trees all day, so trees developed rough bark to protect themselves. This story also led to the naming of the woodpecker family: Picidae.

The green woodpecker rarely drums (except to make nest holes in trees) and instead eats ants on the ground.

The pileated woodpecker's name, referencing its red crest, is derived from the Latin word *pileatus*, meaning "capped."

The bronze statue known as the Capitoline Wolf depicts the orphaned Romulus and Remus rescued by a she-wolf.

Also from Roman mythology comes the story of the woodpecker's involvement in the early lives of Romulus and Remus, twin sons of the god Mars who were taken from their mother and cast into the Tiber River. Rescued and fed by a wolf and a woodpecker, the twins later became the founders of Rome, and wolves and woodpeckers became sacred animals to the Romans. Throughout ancient Italy, woodpeckers represented guardianship, and they were revered in early Roman Catholic artwork because their steady drumming symbolized continual prayer.

In folklore, the woodpecker is sometimes associated with thunder and lighting. In southern Europe, birds such as the middle spotted and Eurasian green woodpeckers were believed to be rainmakers—and their drumming a call for rainstorms. In the Americas, however, woodpeckers were seen as protectors against bad weather, since they warned people of coming storms.

For many **indigenous** peoples of North America, woodpeckers are symbols of home and family. A Pawnee Indian tale tells how the turkey and the woodpecker held a contest to see who was the better protector of humans. The turkey, a bird that lays many eggs, believed she was the

most capable caregiver, as she watched over many young at once. But the woodpecker believed she better protected her young by cloistering them inside the trunk of a tree. At the end of the year, the turkey had lost most of her young to predators, but the woodpecker's babies were still safe. This proved that the woodpecker was the better protector, and she was given the task of watching over humans.

As nature's drummer, the woodpecker is also associated with many American Indians' traditions of drumming. Many tribes believe drumming is a way of communicating

In Italian artist Benvenuto Tisi's Picus Transformed into a Bird, *the figure of Picus is shown sprouting wings and starting to fly.*

The woodpecker symbolized war to the Mississippian culture (A.D. 800–1500), and its image appeared on their armor.

with the spirit world. Thus, the woodpecker is often seen as a messenger, or prophet, connected to the spirit world.

Spiritual animals are often represented in artwork and costumes. In Florida, **archaeologists** have discovered early hairpins bearing woodpecker designs. The knife-shaped objects, made from tortoise shell, have carved woodpecker heads featuring gold, silver, or copper eyes. Researchers believe the pins, which date back to the 16th century, were used to adorn American Indian headbands or turbans.

Woodpecker scalps were also valued among American Indians of the northwestern United States. In what is now northern California, the Atsugewi and Shasta Indians used jewelry, precious stones, and bright red woodpecker scalps as money. The Maidu and Yurok Indians of the same area also used woodpecker scalps in sacred headdresses, sometimes including up to 70 red scalps—alternating them with the white fur of deer bellies—in each headdress. Such **regalia** is rarely found today and is highly valued by museums and collectors.

Ceremonial and everyday objects such as amulets and charms, pottery, and even ax handles that utilized woodpecker feathers have been found throughout the

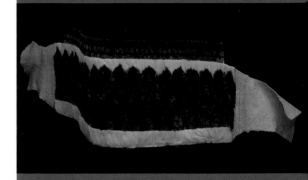

The Karuk (neighbors of the Shasta and Yurok) made woodpecker headdresses for a special ceremony called the Jump Dance.

The red-necked woodpecker was featured on Suriname's 5 gulden note (a form of its guilder currency) in the early 2000s.

Woodpecker calls vary, from the squeak of the downy woodpecker to the shrill squawk of the black-headed woodpecker.

southeastern U.S. Some of these items, such as pendants made of shell and carved with images of woodpeckers, date back nearly 1,000 years and have been found in Tennessee, Alabama, and Mississippi. Scientists agree that most American artifacts bearing images of woodpeckers are based on the likenesses of ivory-billed woodpeckers, which were once abundant across the country.

Contemporary images of woodpeckers can be found all around the world. Red-headed and Gila woodpeckers have appeared on U.S. postage stamps; the green woodpecker is featured on a coin from the Republic of Moldova, a country in southeastern Europe; and the red-necked woodpecker could be found on the former paper currency of the South American country of Suriname. The northern flicker (also known as the yellowhammer) was selected as the official state bird of Alabama in 1927. It has since appeared on commemorative postage stamps and state license plates.

Woodpeckers have found their way into fiction as well. British artist Brian Wildsmith's 1971 children's book *The Owl and the Woodpecker* today remains a favorite tale of rivals becoming friends. More recently, a series of books featuring the character of Professor Woodpecker presents fun stories and activities on a variety of topics, from baseball cards and toy trains to vegetable gardening—all explained by a pileated woodpecker wearing a red bow tie. Professor Woodpecker creators Lee Thompson and Stanley Hill also host an interactive Professor Woodpecker Web site where visitors can read stories and color pictures.

The best-known fictional woodpecker, however, is Woody Woodpecker, the mischievous bird created by Walter Lantz and first voiced by Mel Blanc for Universal Studios in 1940. Woody was first featured in the cartoon *Knock, Knock*, in which he pestered a pair of vacationing pandas. Through decades of change at Universal Studios, Lantz and his successors kept Woody in the spotlight by featuring the tall-haired bird in nearly 200 other cartoons, television shows, movies, and video games until recently. Woody became so important to Universal's history that the studio named Woody Woodpecker the official mascot of the Universal Studios Theme Parks. Woody was also honored with a star on the Hollywood Walk of Fame in 1990. Woody is known for his signature laugh, which his creator modeled after the call of the acorn woodpecker.

This stamp was created in honor of Alabama's sesqui-centennial, or the 150th anniversary of its statehood.

Northern flickers that live in the eastern U.S. are called yellow-shafted flickers for their coloration.

CLINGING TO THE FUTURE

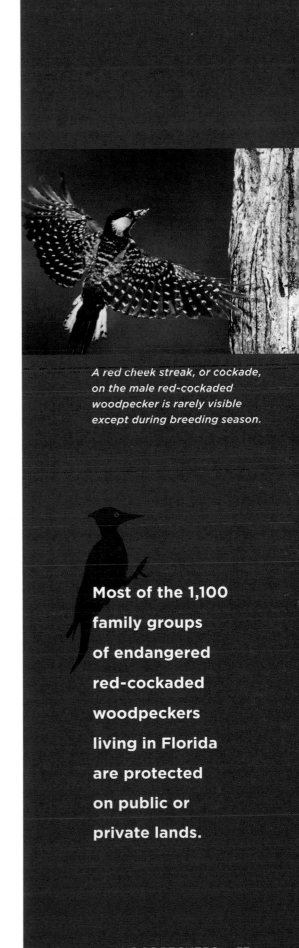

A ll birds likely **evolved** from hollow-boned reptiles that existed millions of years ago. Fossils of feathered, birdlike dinosaurs—such as *Archaeopteryx* and *Xiaotingia zhengi*—that lived 150 to 155 million years ago point to possible links between reptiles and the first true birds. Scientists believe the first true woodpeckers appeared about 50 million years ago in the Northern Hemisphere, and more species evolved in the Southern Hemisphere about 25 million years ago. No fossils of prehistoric woodpeckers larger than the imperial woodpecker have ever been found, suggesting that, unlike many birds, woodpeckers have remained relatively unchanged in size since their earliest days on Earth.

The feathers of modern woodpeckers appear to have remained the same over millions of years as well. Research on fossilized feathers conducted at Yale University by a team led by Jakob Vinther revealed in 2008 that melanosomes (substances that provide color in living organisms) preserved in prehistoric woodpecker feathers were identical to those in modern woodpecker feathers. Vinther and others studying woodpecker feather

A red cheek streak, or cockade, on the male red-cockaded woodpecker is rarely visible except during breeding season.

Most of the 1,100 family groups of endangered red-cockaded woodpeckers living in Florida are protected on public or private lands.

Food shortages or overpopulated habitats cause black-backed woodpeckers to travel far south of their normal range to breed.

The American and Eurasian three-toed woodpeckers and the black-backed woodpecker have only one back toe on each foot.

fossils from Brazil noted the same "ladder" pattern that appears on woodpeckers today.

Migration is a behavior exhibited by a variety of animals, including many woodpecker species. The need for food is what drives woodpecker migration. Larger woodpecker species, such as pileated woodpeckers and northern flickers, need more food than most winter habitats can provide, so these birds fly south, where food is more plentiful. Likewise, since sapsuckers feed on sap that flows from growing trees, these birds must also migrate to warmer climates in the winter.

A few species migrate for different purposes. A number of woodpecker species have **adapted** to seek food provided by humans. Woodpeckers find blocks of waxy animal fat called suet and black oil sunflower desirable, and many bird lovers provide feeders filled with these foods in the winter to attract woodpeckers. Some species will never approach urban areas, but downy woodpeckers in particular can be **conditioned** to regularly visit feeders. Another example of conditioning is evidenced in the behavior of the rare black-backed woodpecker of the western U.S. Scientists recently discovered that these birds have become conditioned to respond to controlled burning activities conducted by forest service programs. The birds travel great distances to locate the remnants of forest fires, feeding on the particular insects, such as wood-boring beetles, that attack burned trees.

A project at the University of Montana at Missoula studies how black-backed woodpeckers choose their peculiar habitats. By monitoring the changing population levels and migration paths of these birds, researchers hope to learn how much burned land and which kinds of burned trees the woodpeckers need to survive. Additionally, individual woodpeckers' nest sites are mapped using **Global Positioning System** (GPS) devices. Land managers are now able to consider the scientists' findings when creating land management plans. Prescribed fire and salvage logging operations may now benefit rather than harm the elusive black-backed woodpeckers.

A similar study has been ongoing at the Rocky Mountain Research Station in Bozeman, Montana. In particular, researchers are studying Lewis's woodpeckers in fire-affected ponderosa pine forests of eight western states. Woodpeckers are considered management indicator species, which means they respond to changes in fire management—too much

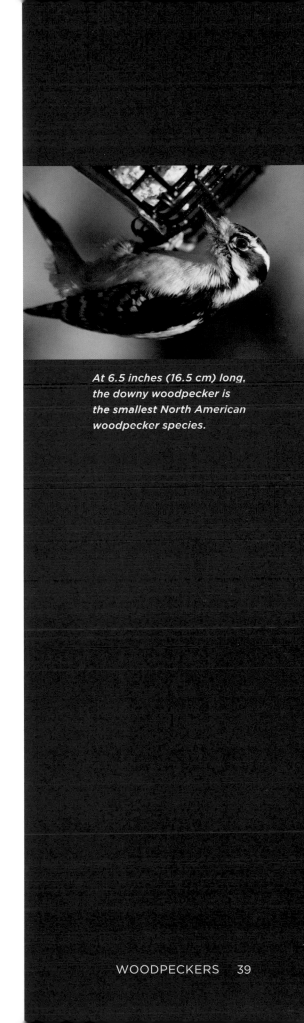

At 6.5 inches (16.5 cm) long, the downy woodpecker is the smallest North American woodpecker species.

The Arizona woodpecker pecks less than other woodpecker species, preferring instead to peel off bark to expose insects.

burning, not enough burning, or burning in the wrong areas—thus helping researchers know whether certain management activities are successful. The Bozeman studies have so far revealed that woodpeckers are more likely to nest in areas burned by wildfire than in areas that were burned deliberately for fire management purposes.

Another type of woodpecker research involves the study of social behavior and family structure in acorn woodpeckers. These woodpeckers live in highly structured community groups that are unique among woodpeckers—and among birds in general. **Ornithologists** at the University of California, Berkeley's Hastings Reservation and Museum of Vertebrate Zoology have been studying acorn woodpeckers since 1971. These birds work together to defend their shared nests and granaries from competing acorn woodpecker communities and predatory birds.

Acorn woodpecker mating is also uniquely shared. The family structure consists of a particular group of brothers, fathers, and sons (called co-breeders) mating only with a selected group of sisters, mothers, and daughters (called joint nesters). The resulting offspring will stay with their family for several years, helping to gather food and feed

younger siblings. These birds, called nonbreeding helpers, can reproduce only if they leave their family and join a rival community to mate with birds that are not related to them. Berkeley's research on these unusual **polygynandrous** (*poh-LIG-in-AN-drus*) mating relationships help natural resource managers develop and implement acorn woodpecker habitat conservation strategies.

Loss of natural habitat may force woodpeckers into urban areas, where they are often unwanted. Sometimes it is necessary to repel woodpeckers that are considered to be harmful or annoying. Woodpeckers are masters at drilling holes in trees, which means they are equally skilled at drilling holes in houses, chimneys, utility poles, and other man-made structures. Woodpeckers may be attracted to just about any structure that stands tall enough and features a surface that the birds' feet can

Acorn woodpeckers feed extensively on young, green acorns before storing ripe acorns for the winter.

Woodpeckers may cause large wounds in trees, which can become infected with fungus or attacked by insects.

grip—including the space shuttle *Discovery*.

In 1995, scientists at the National Aeronautics and Space Administration (NASA) discovered that northern flickers had drilled about 200 holes into the foam insulation surrounding *Discovery*'s fuel tank, causing a delay in the scheduled launch of the shuttle. Following repairs, the flickers were kept from returning to the site by a number of common deterrent methods. Since all woodpeckers in America are protected from certain forms of control under the Migratory Bird Act of 1918, sound devices, mirrors, and fake owls are typically used to scare away unwanted birds.

Woodpecker habitat is often destroyed by urban development and agriculture, and the widespread use of chemicals on crops often devastates woodpecker food sources. When such losses occur, woodpeckers must compete with humans for living space. While most woodpecker species exist in healthy numbers, many have been displaced and must struggle to survive in developed areas. Such effort often leads to starvation, inability to nest, and predation. Continued research on and education about the needs and habits of woodpeckers will be essential to the preservation of these amazing birds.

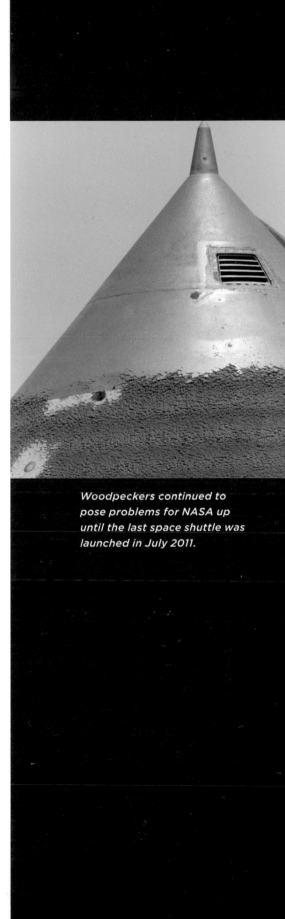

Woodpeckers continued to pose problems for NASA up until the last space shuttle was launched in July 2011.

ANIMAL TALE: WOODPECKER'S REWARD

According to many American Indians, the woodpecker is a helpful bird, as it contributes to the health of forests. This tale from the Lenape, or Delaware, Indians of the northeastern U.S. tells how the woodpecker discovered the favorite food of its relative, the sapsucker.

One particularly hot day, Sugar Maple felt an itch under his bark. Insects had infested his trunk. As the days passed, and the sun burned hotter, the insects and their larvae grew more abundant, and Sugar Maple's itching became unbearable.

"Please help me," Sugar Maple called down to Weasel, who was burrowing under his roots. "Use your sharp claws to relieve me of the insects squirming under my bark."

"I am too busy," replied Weasel as he continued to gather worms from the earth.

Sugar Maple next turned to Beaver, who was using his sharp teeth to cut down a slender sapling nearby. "Please," he begged, "use your long teeth to relieve me of this itching."

"I am too busy," Beaver said and then carried away the sapling in his mouth.

Sugar Maple was in agony as the insects and larvae burrowing tunnels beneath his bark tickled and prickled his flesh. When he saw Porcupine ambling by, looking very unbusy, Sugar Maple called down to him. "Please use your sharp quills to relieve me of these horrid insects," he begged.

Quickening his pace, Porcupine said, "I am too busy." And then he disappeared under a blackberry bush.

Finally, Sugar Maple called out to all the songbirds in his branches, "Please help me!"

They were willing to try, but they could do nothing for Sugar Maple. "We are sorry," said Sparrow, Warbler,

Bluebird, and the others, "but we cannot reach under your bark with our small beaks."

"Oh," moaned Sugar Maple. "I will go mad!"

Then Woodpecker alighted on Sugar Maple's tallest branch. "You seem troubled," Woodpecker said.

"Yes," cried Sugar Maple, and he told Woodpecker his tale of woe.

"I will help you," said Woodpecker. He began chipping away bits of Sugar Maple's bark to reach the insects and larvae squirming under the surface. In less than an hour, Woodpecker had gobbled up every last pest.

"Thank you!" Sugar Maple said. "You have saved me from madness, and for that I will share a delicious secret with you." Woodpecker eagerly listened as Sugar Maple explained: "Fly down near the bottom of my trunk and drill a hole through my bark and deep into my flesh."

Woodpecker did as he was instructed, and in a few moments, sweet sap began to flow from the hole. Woodpecker used his tongue to lap up the sugary liquid. "This is delicious!" Woodpecker exclaimed. "But I am so full of insects I cannot eat another bite."

"Come back later," said Sugar Maple. "Because you were so helpful to me, you and your family are welcome to drink my sap any time you wish."

Woodpecker smiled and flew away, but he soon returned with his cousin. "Taste it," Woodpecker told his cousin. "You will be surprised and delighted."

And Woodpecker's cousin was delighted. As he lapped up the oozing sweetness, he smiled, and Sugar Maple's sap dripped down his beak and covered his plumage. And to this day, Woodpecker's cousin, Yellow-bellied Sapsucker—whose belly is the color of maple sap—eats Sugar Maple's golden treat every chance he gets.

GLOSSARY

adapted – changed to improve its chances of survival in its environment

archaeologists – people who study human history by examining ancient peoples and their artifacts

camouflage – the ability to hide, due to coloring or markings that blend in with a given environment

conditioned – made to respond or behave in a certain way as a result of training

ecosystems – communities of organisms that live together in environments

egg tooth – a hard, toothlike tip of a young bird's beak or a young reptile's mouth, used only for breaking through its egg

evolved – gradually developed into a new form

extinct – having no living members

fledge – to grow feathers necessary for flight

Global Positioning System – a system of satellites, computers, and other electronic devices that work together to determine the location of objects or living things that carry a trackable device

indigenous – originating in a particular region or country

insulate – to protect from the loss of heat

migrate – to undertake a regular, seasonal journey from one place to another and then back again

mortality rate – the number of deaths in a certain area or period

mythology – a collection of myths, or popular, traditional beliefs or stories that explain how something came to be or that are associated with a person or object

neutralize – to make ineffective or harmless

ornithologists – scientists who study birds and their lives

plumage – the entire feathery covering of a bird

polygynandrous – a type of relationship in which a female pairs with several males, each of whom also pairs with several different females

regalia – the ceremonial clothing of a particular group, tribe, or culture

SELECTED BIBLIOGRAPHY

Backhouse, Frances. *Woodpeckers of North America.* Richmond Hill, Ont.: Firefly Books, 2009.

Bannick, Paul. *The Owl and the Woodpecker: Encounters with North America's Most Iconic Birds.* Seattle: Mountaineers Books, 2008.

Gosler, Andrew. *Birds of the World: A Photographic Guide.* Richmond Hill, Ont.: Firefly Books, 2007.

Lehnhausen, William A. "Woodpeckers." Alaska Department of Fish & Game. http://www.adfg.state .ak.us/pubs/notebook/bird/woodpeck.php.

Seattle Audubon Society. "BirdWeb." http://seattleaudubon .org/birdweb.

Snyder, Noel F. R., David E. Brown, and Kevin B. Clark. *The Travails of Two Woodpeckers: Ivory-Bills and Imperials.* Albuquerque: University of New Mexico Press, 2009.

Flying debris indicates that a woodpecker is hard at work constructing the entrance tunnel to its nest.

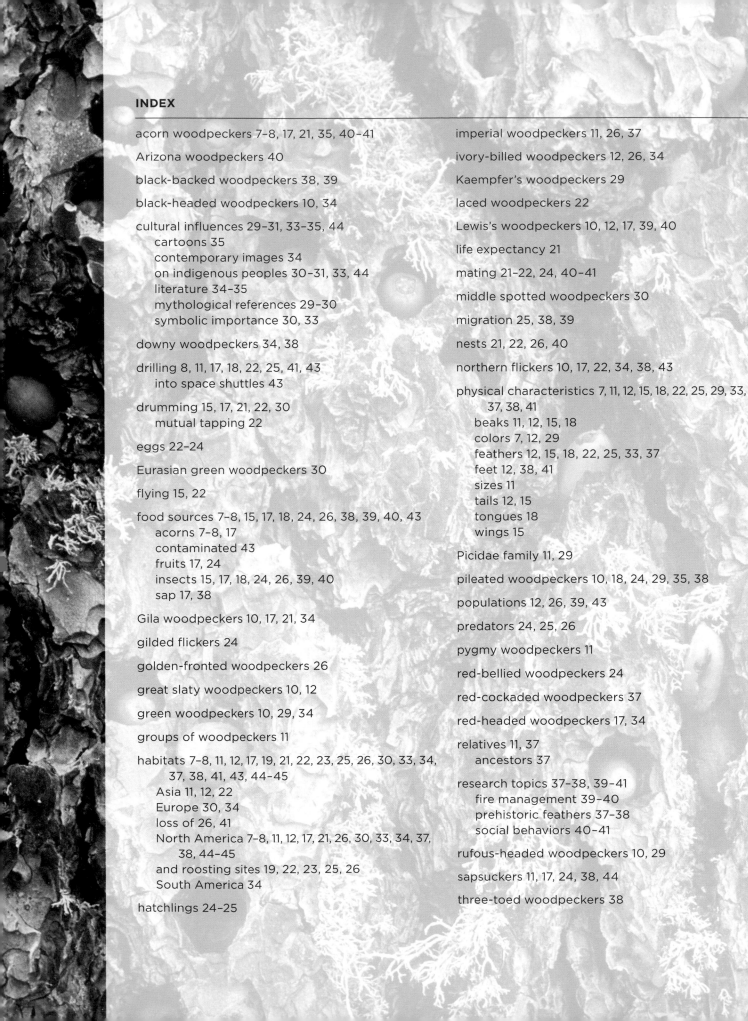

INDEX